SOCIAL MEDIA MARKETING FOR RESTAURANTS

PROVEN TIPS AND STRATEGIES TO BUILD YOUR ONLINE PRESENCE AND ATTRACT MORE CUSTOMERS

RESTAURANT MARKETING BLUEPRINT
BOOK 2

JON NELSEN

DO SOCIAL SMARTER, LLC
marketing   est 2017

Social Media Marketing for Restaurants: Proven Tips and Strategies to Build Your Online Presence and Attract More Customers

Copyright © 2024 by Jon Nelsen

All rights reserved.

Disclaimer Notice:

Please note the information contained within this document is for educational and entertainment purposes only. All effort has been executed to present accurate, up to date, reliable, complete information. No warranties of any kind are declared or implied. Readers acknowledge that the author is not engaged in the rendering of legal, financial, medical or professional advice. The content within this book has been derived from various sources. Please consult a licensed professional before attempting any techniques outlined in this book.

By reading this document, the reader agrees that under no circumstances is the author responsible for any losses, direct or indirect, that are incurred as a result of the use of the information contained within this document, including, but not limited to, errors, omissions, or inaccuracies.

This book is written for entertainment purposes only. The statements made in this book do not necessarily reflect the present market at the time of reading or current views of the author. Furthermore, the author accepts no responsibility for actions taken by the reader as a result of information presented in this book.

No part of this book may be reproduced in any form or by any electronic or mechanical means, including information storage and retrieval systems, without written permission from the author, except for the use of brief quotations in a book review.

CONTENTS

Introduction — 1

1. Understanding Social Media's Role in Restaurant Success — 6
   Why Social Media Is the Secret Ingredient to Thriving in Today's Competitive Market

2. Building a Winning Social Media Strategy — 21
   Create a Clear, Actionable Plan That Drives Real Results

3. Creating Scroll-Stopping Content — 33
   Attract Diners with Irresistible Photos, Videos, and Stories

4. Growing Your Audience Organically — 47
   Build a Loyal Following Without Spending a Fortune

5. Running Paid Social Media Campaigns — 58
   Maximize ROI with Targeted Ads That Drive Reservations

6. Managing Your Restaurant's Online Reputation — 71
   Turn Social Media Feedback Into Positive Relationships

7. Sustaining Long-Term Social Media Success — 82
   Keep Your Restaurant Relevant in an Ever-Changing Digital World

Conclusion — 94

INTRODUCTION

A restaurant isn't just a place to eat; it's an experience, a connection, a story. In today's world, those stories unfold as much online as they do at the table. Social media has transformed how we discover new flavors, share meals, and decide where to dine next. For restaurants, it's no longer optional to have an online presence —it's essential. But how do you move beyond simply being present and start truly engaging with your audience? That's the challenge this book will help you tackle.

Imagine a diner scrolling through Instagram, pausing at a perfectly captured image of a dish that looks both mouthwatering and approachable. They click through to your profile, read your story, and decide they *have* to visit this weekend. That's the power of social media when used effectively—not just posting pretty pictures but creating a dialogue, a relationship, a reason to choose your restaurant over countless others.

The truth is, most restaurant owners and managers

already know they should be active on social media. The real question is how to stand out in a sea of hashtags, filters, and algorithms. The answer lies in strategy. It's not about doing more; it's about doing it right. From understanding which platforms matter most to your audience to creating content that resonates and sparks action, this book will show you how to make every post count.

What makes social media such a game-changer for restaurants? It levels the playing field. Small, independent eateries can now compete with big chains by leveraging authentic storytelling and local connections. Platforms like TikTok and Instagram allow you to turn your culinary artistry into shareable moments. Meanwhile, tools like Facebook and Google enable you to target precisely the customers who are most likely to fall in love with your menu.

But the opportunity comes with challenges. Algorithms reward consistency and creativity, and trends shift quickly. What worked last month might feel outdated today. That's why understanding the foundations of a solid social media strategy is key—not just to keep up, but to get ahead. You'll learn how to align your social media goals with your business objectives, ensuring that every post, story, and comment drives real results.

Social media isn't just about marketing; it's about connection. Diners want more than great food—they want to know the people and passion behind it. Sharing your story authentically creates bonds that go far beyond a one-time reservation. Whether it's highlighting the craftsmanship in your kitchen, the vibrant energy of your dining room, or the community you serve, this book will help you showcase what makes your restaurant unique.

Throughout the chapters ahead, you'll find practical tips and proven strategies drawn from some of the best minds in marketing. You'll explore how to master food photography, craft scroll-stopping videos, and use hashtags to amplify your reach. You'll see how micro-influencers can introduce your restaurant to new audiences and learn how to turn feedback—both positive and negative—into opportunities for growth.

This isn't just a guide to social media; it's a roadmap for building meaningful relationships in a digital age. Whether you're a seasoned operator looking to refine your approach or a newcomer hoping to make a splash, you'll find the tools you need to thrive in today's fast-paced, ever-evolving online landscape.

At its heart, this book is about helping you connect with the diners who will fall in love with your food, your story, and your brand. Social media is the bridge that makes those connections possible. Let's cross it together, one post, one story, one interaction at a time. Welcome to the future of restaurant marketing—it's going to be delicious.

Turn casual diners into loyal fans with Do Social Smarter's proven system to grow your customer base, boost reviews, and drive foot traffic effortlessly.

Visit DoSocialSmarter.com today and discover how to keep your seats full and your competition behind.

DO SOCIAL SMARTER, LLC

marketing　　　　　　　　　　est. 2017

CHEAPTRIVIA.COM

BOOST REVENUE WITH TRIVIA

Revitalize Your Bar or Restaurant with Thrilling Trivia Nights!

- **Weekly trivia questions & answers**
- Boost revenue by thousands
- Enhance customer retention and loyalty
- **Social Posts and Posters available**
- Continuous customer service and support

CHAPTER 1
UNDERSTANDING SOCIAL MEDIA'S ROLE IN RESTAURANT SUCCESS

WHY SOCIAL MEDIA IS THE SECRET INGREDIENT TO THRIVING IN TODAY'S COMPETITIVE MARKET

Social media has become more than just a tool for sharing—it is now one of the most powerful ways for restaurants to connect, engage, and thrive in a competitive market. The way people discover where to eat has changed dramatically. A quick glance at Instagram, a short video on TikTok, or a glowing recommendation on Facebook can influence a diner's decision far more than a traditional ad. For restaurants, understanding how to harness this potential is no longer optional; it's the secret ingredient to long-term success.

Today, the decision to dine out often begins long before someone steps through the door. A potential customer might scroll through an enticing feed of dishes, read reviews from other diners, or watch a chef bring a dish to life. Each interaction tells a story, and every restaurant now has the chance to write its own through social media. Unlike the expensive ads or billboards of the past, platforms like Instagram and Facebook offer a direct way to engage with the audience you care most about, all while letting your unique style and voice shine.

Not all platforms are created equal, though, and each one brings its own strengths. Instagram thrives on visual storytelling, turning dishes into experiences. Facebook helps build communities, where fans can engage in conversations and share their experiences. TikTok, with its rapid-fire content, reaches younger audiences hungry for creativity and authenticity. The challenge isn't being everywhere but knowing where to focus. By choosing the right platforms, restaurants can create connections that feel personal, meaningful, and memorable.

Success in social media also depends on clear goals. Are you looking to attract more diners? Build a loyal community? Showcase your chef's creativity? Setting those objectives is like choosing the perfect recipe—it guides every ingredient and every step. Once those goals are in place, the path forward becomes clearer, whether it's crafting posts that spark curiosity, responding to customer comments with warmth, or sharing behind-the-scenes moments that humanize your brand.

Restaurants that succeed on social media also know how to watch and learn. The most successful campaigns aren't built in isolation—they take inspiration from others. Whether it's seeing how a competitor uses humor to connect with followers or recognizing trends that align with your brand, paying attention to what works for others can spark ideas that feel fresh and relevant. Even more importantly, looking outward helps you spot the gaps, those opportunities to stand out and show why your restaurant is truly unique.

At its core, social media isn't just about promoting a business; it's about fostering relationships. Restaurants have always thrived on community, and these platforms offer a way to extend that connection far beyond the walls of your dining room. It's about showing people what makes your restaurant special, not in a polished, corporate way, but through real, human stories. That's what keeps customers coming back—and brings in new ones eager to be part of the experience.

Social media offers endless opportunities for restaurants ready to embrace its power. By the time you understand how to align your efforts with the right platforms and goals, you'll find that social media isn't a challenge to tackle but a stage to shine on. It's where diners discover, engage, and fall in love with the stories you tell. And it all starts with knowing how to use it to show the heart of your restaurant.

Why Social Media Matters for Restaurants

A few years ago, a small, family-owned pizzeria in a quiet corner of Brooklyn was struggling to bring in customers. They had great food, but with countless other options nearby, they couldn't seem to stand out. Then, their teenage son took charge of their Instagram account. He started posting photos of their wood-fired pies, their cozy dining area, and, most importantly, their family working together behind the counter. The account grew steadily, and soon, their tables were packed every night. What changed? Their story and their food had been great all along, but now they were showing it to the right audience, in the right way.

The way diners decide where to eat has shifted dramatically. A few decades ago, most people relied on word of mouth or advertisements in the local paper. Today, more than 90% of people look up a restaurant online before visiting, according to a survey by OpenTable. Social media plays a massive role in those searches, with Instagram and TikTok leading the way for food lovers seeking inspiration. **If your restaurant isn't visible online, you're essentially invisible to a large portion of your potential audience.**

One reason social media is so effective for restaurants is its visual nature. Food is a universal language, and platforms like Instagram thrive on stunning visuals that grab attention. A vibrant photo of a steaming bowl of ramen or a slow-motion video of a gooey chocolate cake being cut can stop someone mid-scroll. **Visual content is twice as likely to be shared on social media than other types of posts, according to a study by HubSpot, which means your most eye-catching** creations have the power to reach audiences far beyond your regular followers.

But it's not just about the visuals. Diners increasingly want to connect with the people behind the food. Carlos Gil, in *The End of Marketing*, explains that brands need to humanize their presence online. For restaurants, this means sharing more than just what's on the menu. Posting about your team, your process, and your community involvement gives your audience reasons to care about your story and not just your dishes. **People are more likely to choose a restaurant they feel connected to, and social media is where those connections are made.**

Beyond building connections, a strong online presence also directly impacts revenue. Consider this: Yelp's 2022 Economic Impact Report found that restaurants with higher engagement on social media often saw increased foot traffic and online orders. For a small business, even a modest uptick in traffic can make a significant difference. Social media creates a feedback loop—strong engagement leads to more visibility, which leads to more customers, which, in turn, drives further engagement. **The cycle feeds itself when done correctly, allowing even small players to compete with larger chains.**

However, succeeding on social media requires understanding how diners use these platforms. While Instagram is excellent for showcasing beautiful photos, TikTok excels at storytelling through quick, relatable videos. Facebook remains a powerful tool for local community engagement and promotions. **Choosing the right platform for your audience and focusing your energy there prevents you from spreading yourself too thin.** It's better to dominate one platform than to have a weak presence on several.

Restaurants that succeed on social media often focus on being consistent and authentic. Instead of trying to mimic trends that don't fit their brand, they lean into what makes them unique. For the Brooklyn pizzeria, it was the warmth of their family. For a local seafood shack, it might be the fresh catch arriving daily from the harbor. **The key is to show what makes your restaurant worth choosing, in a way that feels honest and engaging.**

Social media isn't just another marketing tool; it's how people find and connect with food in today's world. If you're not actively participating, you're missing out on opportunities to showcase your best qualities and invite diners to your table. By using the platforms where your audience already spends their time, sharing what makes your restaurant special, and engaging authentically, you can transform your online presence into a steady stream of new customers—and loyal fans.

Identifying the Right Platforms for Your Restaurant

What makes a diner choose one restaurant over

another when scrolling through their phone? It's often as simple as how well the restaurant shows up on the platforms they're already using. Social media has made it easier than ever to connect with potential customers, but not all platforms work the same way. Picking the right one can make the difference between attracting a steady stream of diners or being overlooked entirely.

Instagram thrives on visuals, making it perfect for restaurants. A well-lit photo of your best dish, a candid shot of your team, or a colorful overhead spread of your menu can capture attention instantly. **Instagram users engage most with posts that are visually appealing and authentic**, according to a 2022 Sprout Social study. Restaurants that use Instagram effectively often see their photos shared widely, increasing their visibility far beyond their existing followers. Adding location tags or hashtags like #FoodieParadise or #YourCityEats helps potential customers find you when they're searching for places to dine.

TikTok, on the other hand, is all about quick, entertaining content. This platform rewards creativity and storytelling over polished production. A short clip showing a chef's unique plating skills, a behind-the-scenes look at your kitchen, or a fun challenge featuring your signature dish can go viral in hours. **TikTok's algorithm is designed to surface content to users who might never have heard of your restaurant but share interests in food, local spots, or trends.** If your target audience skews younger, focusing on TikTok is often worth the effort, as the platform's reach among users aged 18–30 is unmatched.

Facebook remains a powerful tool for connecting with local communities. Its events feature allows you to promote happy hours, live music, or special dinners directly to people nearby. It's also one of the best platforms for reviews, where satisfied customers can share their experiences. **Facebook's value lies in its ability to foster long-term loyalty**, with tools like messaging, group pages, and posts that spark conversations with your audience.

Choosing the right platform depends heavily on understanding your customer base. A trendy bistro targeting Millennials might focus on Instagram and TikTok, while a family-friendly diner with strong community ties might prioritize Facebook. Demographic research is key here. **Look at your existing customers: their age, habits, and interests can help you decide where to focus your time.** Once you know who you're trying to reach, you can align your content strategy with the platforms where they spend their time.

Spreading yourself across every platform can dilute your efforts. It's better to excel on one or two platforms than to have a weak presence everywhere. **Start with the platforms where you're most likely to connect with your audience, and build a strong presence there before branching out.** By concentrating your efforts, you ensure that your message stays consistent and impactful.

Social media gives restaurants something traditional marketing never could: direct engagement. There's no need to go through the hoops of expensive ad buys or hope your message reaches the right audience. With platforms like Instagram, TikTok, and Facebook, you're speaking directly to potential diners. This kind of access is invaluable, especially for smaller restaurants competing against big-name chains with huge marketing budgets. **Social media levels the playing field by allowing you to showcase what makes your restaurant unique without needing a massive investment.**

By focusing on the platforms that work best for your audience and staying consistent in your messaging, you can transform casual online browsers into loyal patrons. Each post, story, or video becomes an invitation—one that brings your brand to life and builds anticipation for the experience only your restaurant can provide.

Setting Clear Goals for Social Media Marketing

"Goals are dreams with deadlines," management expert Diana Scharf Hunt once said. In the world of social media marketing, this quote holds true for restaurants striving to stand out online. Without clear objectives, it's easy to get lost in the constant churn of posts, likes, and algorithms. But when you define your purpose, every effort—every photo, comment, and video—has meaning. Clear goals aren't just helpful;

they're essential for turning casual social media use into a powerful tool for growth.

Success looks different depending on your restaurant's needs. Some businesses want to focus on **building awareness**, ensuring as many people as possible know about their location and offerings. Others might prioritize **engagement**, creating a loyal community that interacts with posts and shares them with friends. Still, others may focus on **direct sales**, driving online orders or bookings. Each of these outcomes requires a distinct strategy, and understanding what success means to you will shape how you approach your content.

Effective goals also need to be measurable. The SMART framework—specific, measurable, achievable, relevant, and time-bound—provides a clear structure for defining what you want to achieve. Instead of saying, "I want more followers," a SMART goal would specify, "Increase Instagram followers by 20% in the next three months through weekly content posts and active engagement." **This clarity helps you track progress and make adjustments when something isn't working.** Measuring results not only keeps you focused but also helps you identify what resonates most with your audience.

Aligning your social media goals with broader business objectives ensures that every post supports your restaurant's overall success. If your goal is to boost weekday reservations, your social media strategy might involve showcasing happy hour specials or limited-time offers during slower hours. If you're aiming to introduce a new menu, you could focus on sharing behind-the-scenes videos of your chef preparing signature dishes. **When social media goals tie directly to your business outcomes, they amplify your efforts, creating tangible results.**

Consistency is another critical component. Social media works best when value is delivered regularly. A page that shares quality content one week but goes silent the next quickly loses its audience's attention. Balancing consistent posts with calls to action keeps your presence active while giving followers a reason to engage. Not every post needs to promote an offer or event. In fact, sprinkling in entertaining, informative, or simply beautiful content helps build trust, making your audience more likely to act when you do include promotional messages. **The key is to focus on the long-term relationship, not just short-term wins.**

Restaurants that thrive on social media often understand the balance between creativity and strategy. For example, a local taco shop might aim to boost awareness by participating in national food holidays like Taco Tuesday, posting fun, themed content while tagging relevant hashtags to attract new followers. At the same time, they might align posts about their catering service with their goal of increasing group orders. By matching creative ideas with strategic intent, the shop turns every post into a step toward its broader goals.

It's also essential to remain flexible. Social media

trends evolve quickly, and rigid plans can leave your content feeling outdated. Monitoring your performance metrics, such as engagement rates and reach, allows you to adjust your goals and tactics as needed. If a particular type of post—like behind-the-scenes videos—consistently outperforms others, doubling down on that format can yield better results. **Flexibility doesn't mean abandoning your goals; it means refining your approach to achieve them more effectively.**

At its core, setting clear goals for social media marketing is about clarity and intention. Without these, even the most creative posts can feel scattered, missing their mark. But when you define success, measure progress, and stay consistent, your social media efforts become more than a task—they become a tool that drives real growth for your restaurant.

Evaluating Competitors and Trends

"The competition is always a click away," social media strategist Carlos Gil reminds us in his book *The End of Marketing*. For restaurants, this couldn't be more accurate. Diners have endless options, and the decision often hinges on how a restaurant presents itself online. By studying what competitors are doing and understanding current trends, you can find your edge and turn it into a competitive advantage. The key isn't just imitation but learning how to stand out while delivering value that resonates with your audience.

Successful restaurants don't just share content—they share the *right* content for their brand. Exploring the social media profiles of your competitors reveals a wealth of information. Notice how they structure their posts, the type of engagement they receive, and which campaigns appear to generate the most excitement. **Pay attention to details like the tone of their captions, the balance between promotional and personal content, and how they respond to comments.** These insights help you identify best practices in your niche while avoiding potential pitfalls.

Trends offer another layer of opportunity. Whether it's participating in viral challenges or utilizing popular hashtags like #FoodieFriday or #EatLocal, staying current helps you remain visible in an ever-changing landscape. **Trendy content often aligns with what people are actively searching for, giving you a chance to reach new audiences.** However, it's vital to adapt trends to suit your brand rather than forcing your content to fit. A high-end steakhouse, for example, might approach a TikTok challenge differently than a casual burger joint, emphasizing sophistication while still engaging in fun ways.

Understanding trends also involves identifying which formats are gaining traction. Reels, Stories, and behind-the-scenes videos are currently dominating platforms like Instagram and TikTok. Competitors who leverage these formats effectively are worth watching. Look at how they incorporate storytelling into their posts or highlight their unique selling points, such as sustainability or locally sourced ingredients. **The more you understand what's working, the better equipped you are to refine your own strategy.**

One of the most powerful ways to differentiate your brand is by identifying what competitors *aren't* doing. If every restaurant in your area is focused on promoting specials, there's an opportunity to highlight the personal stories of your team instead. If competitors rarely interact with followers in comments, doubling down on engagement can set you apart. **Gaps in their strategy are chances for you to shine in ways that matter to your audience.**

Brand identity plays a crucial role here. It's tempting to copy what appears to work for others, but your audience wants authenticity. Study competitors' personal branding, but adapt it to reflect your values and vision. For instance, if a nearby restaurant excels at humorous content but that doesn't align with your upscale image, you might focus on educational posts about your wine pairings or the artistry behind your dishes. **The goal is to understand what resonates while staying true to your restaurant's character.**

Social media trends aren't just about following the latest buzz; they're about staying connected to what people care about. If local farm-to-table dining is gaining attention, sharing your partnerships with nearby growers can create a deeper connection with your audience. Similarly, if sustainability is trending, highlighting eco-friendly initiatives like compostable packaging or waste reduction can help differentiate your brand. **By aligning with meaningful movements, you position your restaurant as relevant and forward-thinking.**

Evaluating competitors and trends isn't a one-time task; it's an ongoing process. Social media evolves quickly, and staying informed ensures you're always a step ahead. By consistently analyzing what others are doing and reflecting on how you can do it differently—or better—you turn observation into action. **Your competitive edge comes not from replicating but from innovating, crafting a strategy that highlights what makes your restaurant truly unique.**

CHAPTER 2
BUILDING A WINNING SOCIAL MEDIA STRATEGY

CREATE A CLEAR, ACTIONABLE PLAN THAT DRIVES REAL RESULTS

Social media success rarely happens by accident. Behind every viral post and thriving account is a strategy built on purpose and precision. Restaurants, in particular, cannot afford to rely on luck. A well-thought-out plan can transform your social media from a simple posting habit into a powerhouse that drives diners through your doors. Without a clear strategy, efforts become scattered, and opportunities are missed. With one, your content, goals, and results align, delivering real outcomes that matter to your business.

Crafting a winning social media strategy begins with understanding your restaurant's unique identity. No two establishments are the same, and your strategy should reflect what sets yours apart. Are you known for upscale dining, a family-friendly atmosphere, or the trendiest dishes in town? Every choice, from your tone of voice to the type of content you create, should tie back to these core attributes. This ensures that your audience recognizes your brand instantly and builds trust with every interaction.

A strong strategy also relies on balance. The content you create must strike the right mix of engaging, educational, and promotional. Overloading your audience with sales pitches can alienate them, while failing to remind them of what you offer leaves money on the table. By designing a thoughtful content plan, you ensure your posts consistently provide value while still supporting your business goals. For example, sharing behind-the-scenes videos builds engagement, while limited-time offers create urgency.

Timing and consistency are just as crucial as the content itself. Social media moves quickly, and even the most compelling post loses impact if it goes unnoticed. That's why an actionable plan includes not just what to post, but when and how often. Regular activity keeps your restaurant top-of-mind for your followers and ensures that your efforts compound over time. A reliable schedule also allows you to capitalize on peak moments, like lunch rushes, holidays, and community events.

No strategy is complete without clear measurements of success. Knowing what to aim for—whether it's more followers, higher engagement, or increased bookings—guides every decision you make. Without defined objectives, even the best ideas risk falling flat. By tying your strategy to specific outcomes, you can track your progress and make informed adjustments along the way.

Building a social media strategy may seem like a daunting task, but it doesn't have to be. It's about creating a plan that serves your restaurant's goals while staying flexible enough to adapt to the ever-changing landscape of digital marketing. With a solid foundation, every post becomes more than just content—it becomes a step toward building a loyal community, attracting new diners, and growing your business in ways you can see and measure.

Crafting Your Brand Voice and Visual Identity

A restaurant's brand is more than its logo or menu—it's the feeling it creates when a guest interacts with it. Take the case of a small diner in New Orleans. Known for its classic gumbo, the diner didn't just post photos of its dishes on Instagram. Instead, it shared stories of the generations-old recipe, coupled with warm, inviting visuals of the family behind the scenes. Over time, it built a brand that wasn't just about food—it was about heritage, warmth, and trust. The result? An audience that didn't just crave the gumbo but felt emotionally tied to the experience the diner promised.

Creating this kind of connection starts with defining your restaurant's tone and personality. Consider what you want people to feel when they think about your establishment. Are you a playful taco stand with bold flavors and brighter-than-life colors, or an intimate bistro offering a refined, cozy atmosphere? The way you describe yourself here will guide everything else—your social media captions, the colors you use, and even the photos you choose to share. Think of this as setting the emotional tone of your brand. It ensures every element of your online presence resonates with your restaurant's core essence.

A cohesive aesthetic is equally important. Consistency across platforms doesn't just make you look polished—it builds trust with your audience. Choose a palette of two or three colors that reflect your restaurant's vibe and stick to them. Pair these with fonts that align with your style. A rustic café might opt for handwritten-style typography, while a sleek, modern sushi bar might use clean, minimalistic typefaces. Your visuals, too, should reinforce your identity. If you're known for fresh, farm-to-table offerings, use natural light and earthy tones to showcase your dishes. Over time, this visual language will become as recognizable as your food.

Humanizing your branding is where the magic happens. People connect with people, not businesses. Introduce your chef sharing tips in short clips or highlight your team celebrating small wins, like a busy Friday night. Let your audience see the people behind the dishes, and show them moments of your restaurant's day-to-day life. This makes your brand approachable, relatable, and ultimately, unforgettable. When diners feel a human connection, they're far more likely to engage with your content and become loyal customers.

It's also crucial to ensure that every element of your branding aligns seamlessly across platforms. The tone and visuals you use on Instagram should feel cohesive with those on TikTok or Facebook. While the content may vary based on the platform's strengths—short, snappy videos for TikTok versus curated photo posts for Instagram—the core identity should remain consistent. This continuity reinforces your brand's professionalism and reliability.

Crafting a brand voice and visual identity is more than an exercise in design; it's a strategy for connection. It ensures every post, comment, and visual you create tells the same story, making it easy for diners to understand who you are and why you matter. The more clearly you communicate your brand, the stronger your restaurant's identity becomes in the minds—and hearts—of your audience.

Creating a Content Calendar That Works

How often do you see a beautifully crafted social media post and wonder if it was pure luck or part of a larger plan? For successful restaurants, it's rarely luck. Behind the scenes, their posts are guided by a well-thought-out content calendar that aligns with their goals, values, and audience preferences. A content calendar is more than a tool; it's a strategy that ensures consistency, builds trust, and helps restaurants stay ahead of trends while saving precious time.

Every content calendar begins with a clear understanding of the key dates that matter to your restaurant and your customers. Major holidays, local festivals, and food-specific celebrations like National Pizza Day or Taco Tuesday are natural opportunities to engage your audience. But a great calendar also highlights your unique promotions, events, or milestones, such as a new menu launch or the anniversary of your restaurant's opening. By planning around these moments, you ensure your content feels timely and relevant, drawing more eyes to your posts.

Balancing your content types is the next essential step. Think of your calendar as a way to create variety while maintaining focus. **Engaging content**, such as behind-the-scenes photos or interactive polls, keeps your followers interested in your restaurant as a personality, not just a business. **Educational posts**, like cooking tips, ingredient stories, or pairing suggestions, position your brand as a knowledgeable and helpful resource. Finally, **promotional content**, such as limited-time offers or special event announcements, drives action. By alternating between these categories, your posts remain fresh while ensuring you're delivering consistent value to your audience.

Templates and scheduling tools can transform content creation from a daunting task into a manageable system. Tools like Buffer or Hootsuite allow you to organize and automate your posts, ensuring that your best ideas are shared at optimal times without last-minute scrambling. Templates, whether for Instagram carousels or Facebook Stories, ensure your visuals stay consistent with your branding while saving hours of design work. The goal is to maximize efficiency without sacrificing quality.

A content calendar becomes even more powerful when it's informed by the needs and desires of your customers. Start by analyzing the posts that get the most engagement—comments, shares, or likes—and look for patterns. Do your followers love posts about seasonal dishes, or are they more responsive to staff shoutouts? Use these insights to tailor your content to what your audience wants, ensuring every post resonates with the people you're trying to attract.

By investing time in creating a value-driven content calendar, you're not just managing your social media—you're shaping the narrative of your restaurant. You're ensuring that every post has a purpose, every image and caption adds to your story, and every promotion fits into a larger strategy. Through thoughtful planning, your social media presence becomes a cohesive extension of your brand, keeping your restaurant top of mind while freeing you to focus on the other parts of your business.

Using Hashtags and Keywords Strategically

"Good hashtags make good neighbors." While Robert Frost never wrote about Instagram, this updated proverb perfectly encapsulates the way hashtags and keywords create connections in the digital world. Imagine a diner scrolling through their feed, searching for a place to celebrate their anniversary. The perfect post, tagged with #BestPizzaNYC and #DateNightEats, appears, and suddenly, the choice is clear. For restaurants, mastering hashtags and keywords isn't optional—it's essential for getting noticed in a sea of content.

Hashtags are the digital bridges between your content and the people who need to see it. The key is choosing ones that resonate with your audience while reflecting your brand. Start by researching hashtags relevant to your niche. Tools like Hashtagify or Instagram's own suggestions can reveal what's trending. Look for tags with high engagement but not so much competition that your post gets buried. **Pair broader tags, like #Foodie, with more specific ones, like #BrooklynBrunch, to maximize both reach and relevance.** These combinations help attract both the general audience and the diners searching locally.

Geo-tags and location-based hashtags are especially valuable for restaurants. If your customers are nearby, use tags like #ChicagoEats or #AustinFoodScene to show off your dishes where they're likely to be discovered. Even on platforms like Instagram Stories, adding a location sticker can increase your visibility to users scrolling through local feeds. Geo-tags not only attract local diners but also give your restaurant credibility by connecting it to the culture and identity of your area.

Captions play a starring role in your posts, and targeted keywords make them perform even better. Incorporating phrases people are likely to search for, such as "vegan-friendly lunch in Portland" or "happy hour deals," can enhance discoverability, especially when paired with location tags. Keywords should flow naturally within the caption rather than feeling forced. **Write captions as if speaking to a regular customer. For example, instead of saying "Spaghetti on special," describe it: "Stop in today for fresh, handmade spaghetti in our classic tomato sauce."** These details not only add warmth but also reflect the kinds of words potential diners might search for online.

While hashtags and keywords help users find your content, overusing them can create the opposite effect. Posts crammed with irrelevant or excessive hashtags can seem spammy, discouraging engagement. A good rule of thumb is to prioritize quality over quantity. Experiment with the number of hashtags you use, keeping in mind that some platforms, like Instagram, allow up to 30, while others, like Twitter, work best with just a few. **Always choose meaningful tags over generic ones to attract the right audience.**

Tracking which hashtags and keywords perform well can make your strategy even more effective. Many platforms provide insights into post engagement, showing how often your content is discovered through specific tags. Use this data to refine your choices over time, focusing on what drives likes, comments, and clicks. **Experiment with new hashtags periodically while retaining those that consistently bring in results.**

Building visibility through hashtags and keywords may seem small, but these tools have the power to create significant opportunities for your restaurant. By being intentional about what you use and how you use it, your posts can rise above the noise, capturing the attention of both loyal patrons and curious new diners. And in the ever-changing landscape of social media, a solid strategy for discovery keeps your restaurant in the spotlight.

Setting Up a Metrics-Driven Feedback Loop

For restaurants, data-driven feedback loops are the secret to turning sporadic posts into a cohesive and effective strategy. Every like, share, and comment is a piece of the puzzle that reveals what resonates with your audience and what doesn't.

To harness this power, begin by defining the most meaningful key performance indicators (KPIs) for your restaurant. Engagement rates, such as likes, comments, and shares, reveal how well your content connects emotionally with your audience. Meanwhile, growth metrics, like new followers or subscribers, indicate your ability to attract fresh eyes to your brand. **Prioritize KPIs that align with your ultimate goals. If your aim is** to increase foot traffic, monitor how many people mention your restaurant online after promotions. If it's brand awareness, impressions and reach will hold more weight.

Tracking these metrics is the next critical step, and this requires consistency. Social media platforms like Instagram, Facebook, and TikTok offer built-in analytics tools that simplify the process. Third-party apps such as Sprout Social or Hootsuite can provide more advanced tracking capabilities. By regularly analyzing your post performance, you'll spot patterns—such as the types of posts that get the most comments or the times of day when engagement peaks. **Use this data to experiment, tweaking your timing, visuals, or captions to refine your approach over time.**

Metrics are also invaluable for measuring the effectiveness of your content mix. Striking the right balance between value-driven and promotional content is a constant challenge, but data helps clarify what your audience prefers. Posts that educate, entertain, or inspire often receive higher engagement, while promotional posts might drive more direct actions like reservations. **Review the performance of these categories side-by-side to ensure you're not overwhelming your followers with sales pitches while still meeting business objectives.**

Adjusting your strategy based on what works—and what doesn't—is where a feedback loop becomes dynamic. When a type of content performs well, analyze why. Did a post include a trending topic or hashtag? Was it a video rather than an image? Conversely, low-performing content offers just as much insight. Was the call to action unclear? Did the caption fail to connect? **Treat each post as an opportunity to learn, iterating based on performance while staying true to your brand identity.**

Beyond guiding your own efforts, metrics also reveal shifts in audience behavior and preferences. For example, if engagement starts to drop on certain platforms, it could signal a need to redirect your focus elsewhere. If short-form videos outperform static images, it's a cue to invest in new types of content creation. Metrics keep you adaptable in a rapidly changing social media landscape, ensuring your strategy remains relevant and effective.

The ultimate goal of metrics-driven feedback is refinement, not perfection. Every piece of data is a stepping stone toward understanding your audience better and crafting a strategy that delivers consistent results. With the right KPIs, regular tracking, and a willingness to adapt, your social media presence can grow stronger and more impactful over time, turning casual followers into loyal diners.

CHAPTER 3
CREATING SCROLL-STOPPING CONTENT
ATTRACT DINERS WITH IRRESISTIBLE PHOTOS, VIDEOS, AND STORIES

Imagine scrolling through your favorite social media platform and pausing at a picture so vivid you can almost taste the food on your screen. What makes you stop? What transforms a simple photo into a powerful connection? For restaurants, mastering the art of scroll-stopping content is no longer optional—it's the key to staying relevant in a crowded digital world. Visual storytelling has the power to attract new diners, build loyalty, and showcase what sets your brand apart, all within the span of a single post.

At the heart of creating engaging content is understanding what your audience craves. It's more than just a perfectly plated dish; it's about capturing moments that evoke emotion and spark conversation. This could be the sizzle of a steak hitting the grill, the laughter of diners enjoying their meal, or a close-up of a decadent dessert ready to be devoured. **Authenticity resonates,**

and content that feels real and unpolished often outperforms those that appear overly curated.

Balance is also essential. Visuals are only part of the equation—your captions and storytelling must work together to complete the narrative. A striking photo may catch attention, but a well-crafted caption with the right keywords and hashtags ensures it reaches the right audience. Videos, too, have become essential in drawing engagement, with platforms like TikTok and Instagram prioritizing dynamic, snackable clips. **Whether it's a behind-the-scenes look at your kitchen or a quick tutorial featuring a signature dish, videos create an opportunity to connect on a deeper level.**

Understanding your platform's unique strengths is crucial. Instagram thrives on high-quality photos and reels, while TikTok rewards creativity and humor. Facebook allows for longer storytelling, making it perfect for highlighting your restaurant's values or community involvement. Crafting content specifically tailored to these platforms increases your chances of resonating with users while keeping them engaged with your brand.

In the world of social media, trends evolve quickly, and staying ahead requires both consistency and flexibility. While your strategy should highlight your brand's identity, it must also adapt to the changing preferences of your audience. This might mean jumping on trending sounds for a reel, experimenting with user-generated content, or collaborating with influencers who align with your restaurant's voice. The most successful strategies strike a balance between being rooted in your core values and remaining agile enough to stay fresh. **When done right, your content doesn't just draw attention—it creates memories that lead to loyal customers.**

Mastering scroll-stopping content is not simply about aesthetics or trends. It's about creating moments that are as irresistible online as your food is in person. By aligning visuals, storytelling, and platform strengths, you can craft posts that not only capture attention but also inspire action. It's this synergy that transforms a casual viewer into a diner, and eventually, into a loyal fan.

Mastering Food Photography for Social Media

On a sunny afternoon in a small café, a food blogger sat by the window, snapping a photo of their latte art with the glow of natural light filtering through the glass. What could have been just another drink on a menu became a work of art that resonated with thousands on social media. The secret? Mastering the balance of light, angle, and composition to turn a simple dish into a visual story that people want to share. This skill has transformed how restaurants present themselves, drawing diners not just for the food but for the experience captured online.

At the core of impactful food photography is lighting. **Natural light is the most accessible and effective tool for creating appetizing images.** Position dishes near a window to capture soft, even light that enhances textures and colors. If natural light isn't an option, inexpensive tools like a ring light or a portable LED panel can mimic its effects, ensuring your photos remain well-lit and inviting. Avoid harsh overhead lighting or direct flash, which can flatten the image and make the food appear unappealing.

Angles play a crucial role in showcasing the best features of your dishes. A bird's-eye view works beautifully for flat-lay compositions, especially when highlighting multiple items like a full table spread. On the other hand, a 45-degree angle often mimics a diner's perspective, making it ideal for capturing the depth of a stacked burger or a frothy cappuccino. **Experiment with angles to find what works best for each dish, keeping in mind that the goal is to emphasize textures and dimensions.**

Props and styling add personality and context to your photos. Simple garnishes like fresh herbs, a drizzle of sauce, or a dusting of powdered sugar can elevate the look of a dish. Backgrounds should complement the food without overpowering it. Rustic wooden boards, neutral-colored plates, or textured linens create depth and warmth without distracting from the subject. **Consistency in props and styling reinforces your restaurant's branding, ensuring each photo feels like a cohesive part of your online presence.**

Smartphones are a game-changer in food photography, offering high-quality cameras that rival professional equipment. Many modern devices come equipped with features like portrait mode and HDR, which help enhance focus and color. Downloading editing apps such as Lightroom Mobile or Snapseed allows you to fine-tune brightness, contrast, and saturation, ensuring the final image matches the dish's true-to-life appeal. **Affordable clip-on lenses can also provide wide-angle or macro capabilities, giving you even more flexibility.**

Authenticity is the thread that ties everything together. Overly staged photos often feel disconnected, while images that capture the essence of your restaurant—whether it's a candid shot of a chef at work or the steam rising from a freshly baked dish—create an emotional connection. **Every photo should tell a story about your restaurant's unique offerings, whether it's the comfort of homemade meals or the excitement of experimental cuisine.**

Beyond aesthetics, think about how your photos align with your audience's expectations. A well-composed image of your signature dish can spark curiosity and attract new diners, while a glimpse of seasonal specials keeps loyal customers engaged. Consider the role your photos play in marketing campaigns, ensuring they align with the tone and message of your overall strategy.

The most effective food photography doesn't just

highlight the dish; it conveys the experience. Through the thoughtful use of lighting, angles, props, and authenticity, each photo becomes an invitation—not just to eat, but to savor the story your restaurant offers.

Leveraging Videos and Stories to Boost Engagement

How is it that a 30-second clip of a sizzling steak or a chef's skilled hands assembling a dish can garner thousands of views while other posts barely gain traction? The answer lies in the unmatched ability of video to captivate and engage. Video content, when crafted thoughtfully, combines motion, sound, and storytelling to create an immersive experience that still images often cannot achieve. Leveraging this dynamic medium is essential for standing out on platforms where attention spans are fleeting.

To create compelling TikToks, Reels, and behind-the-scenes clips, **focus on storytelling that highlights the personality of your restaurant.** A behind-the-scenes look at your kitchen, for instance, offers viewers a glimpse into the craftsmanship behind their favorite dishes. Short, punchy clips that showcase your team's personality, like a chef flipping a pan or a barista perfecting latte art, can humanize your brand while drawing in an audience. Keep these videos authentic and engaging by focusing on real moments rather than overly produced content. Apps like InShot or CapCut make it simple to edit videos with transitions, text overlays, and music, keeping your content polished yet approachable.

Stories on platforms like Instagram and Facebook offer a unique way to connect with followers in real-time. Use polls, questions, and countdowns to interact directly with your audience. **Polls are particularly effective for gathering quick feedback**, such as which dessert flavor to feature next or opinions on upcoming specials. Countdown stickers can generate anticipation for events, promotions, or new menu items. Real-time updates, like sharing a freshly plated dish or the arrival of a seasonal ingredient, add immediacy and excitement, encouraging your audience to stay tuned for more.

Repurposing content across multiple platforms extends its lifespan and maximizes its reach. A short clip designed for TikTok can be shared as a Reel on Instagram or edited into a teaser for Stories. **Be mindful of the platform's unique audience and format requirements.** While TikTok thrives on trends and humor, Instagram Reels may require a more polished aesthetic. Facebook audiences might prefer slightly longer videos with more context. Adapting the same content for different platforms ensures consistency in messaging while tailoring the presentation to meet the expectations of each audience.

Understanding and optimizing for platform algorithms is key to boosting visibility. Algorithms often prioritize video content that encourages engagement, such as shares, comments, and watch time. **Hook your viewers within the first three seconds** to keep them watching; a dynamic intro or an intriguing question can work wonders here. Adding subtitles ensures accessibility and increases watch time, as many users view videos with the sound off. Leverage trending sounds and hashtags relevant to your restaurant or theme, as these can increase your content's discoverability.

Quality trumps quantity, but technical aspects like resolution and framing cannot be ignored. Shooting in 1080p or higher ensures your videos look sharp on any device. Vertical framing is best for platforms like Instagram and TikTok, while a 16:9 aspect ratio works well for YouTube and Facebook. Keep your lighting consistent, using natural light or affordable ring lights to make colors pop and food look its best. Clear visuals paired with crisp audio enhance the viewer's experience, ensuring your message resonates.

The key to successful video content lies in its ability to evoke emotion, whether it's excitement, curiosity, or nostalgia. A quick clip of your chef's favorite recipe can transport viewers into the heart of your restaurant, while a customer's enthusiastic reaction to trying a dish offers social proof that words alone cannot convey. Video isn't just a marketing tool—it's a medium to build relationships, tell your story, and invite your audience to be part of the experience.

Incorporating User-Generated Content

How often do you see someone snap a photo of their meal before taking the first bite? In today's social media-driven world, diners have become your restaurant's most influential marketers, creating content that feels authentic and relatable to potential customers. When diners post about their experiences, whether it's a beautifully plated dish or a cozy corner of your restaurant, they provide an invaluable endorsement that no ad campaign can replicate. User-generated content (UGC) is more than just free marketing; it's a trust-building tool that amplifies your reach and strengthens your brand's connection with its audience.

Encouraging diners to share their experiences begins with creating an environment that inspires them to pick up their phones. **Make your space and food visually inviting, and highlight moments that feel worthy of a share.** A unique wall mural, carefully crafted cocktails, or playful presentations of dishes can naturally prompt your customers to post photos or videos. You can also leave subtle reminders on tables or menus, suggesting diners use a branded hashtag when sharing. For example, a hashtag like #EatsAt[YourRestaurant] can unify customer posts and make them easy to find.

When customers share their content, acknowledge and celebrate it by reposting on your social media channels. **Always credit the original creator to show respect for their contribution and build goodwill.** Reposting demonstrates that your restaurant values its community and fosters a sense of belonging among your customers. This strategy also increases the likelihood of others sharing their experiences, knowing they might be featured on your account. Tools like Instagram's built-in reposting feature or third-party apps make it simple to share UGC while maintaining high-quality visuals.

Creating contests is another effective way to encourage UGC while generating excitement about your restaurant. **Photo challenges, where customers share pictures of their favorite dish or unique dining experience for a chance to win a discount or gift card, are particularly engaging.** Pair these contests with a dedicated hashtag to make entries easier to track and to build momentum. The contest itself becomes an event that customers are eager to join, and it provides you with a steady stream of content to showcase. Remember to set clear guidelines and keep the tone playful to ensure the process feels fun rather than transactional.

Hashtags serve as the cornerstone of organizing and promoting UGC campaigns. **Choose hashtags that reflect your brand's identity while being easy to remember and use.** For example, a pizza restaurant might use #SliceOfHappiness, while a fine dining establishment could opt for #DineWithElegance. Encourage diners to include these hashtags in their posts, making it easier for you to find and engage with their content. Local hashtags can also help your posts reach audiences in your area, bringing in potential customers who are nearby and looking for dining options.

To maximize the impact of UGC, integrate it into your broader marketing strategy. **Feature top posts on your website, in newsletters, or even in printed materials within your restaurant.** Highlighting real experiences from real people lends credibility to your brand, showing potential customers that others love dining with you. UGC can also serve as inspiration for your own content, providing insight into what resonates most with your audience.

The beauty of UGC lies in its ability to humanize your brand. It shifts the focus from polished advertising to real moments shared by genuine fans of your restaurant. By fostering and curating UGC, you're not just expanding your content library—you're building a community of advocates who share your passion and help spread your message.

Balancing Authenticity and Professionalism

How can you connect with your audience in a way that feels both genuine and trustworthy? The balance between showing the human side of your business and maintaining a professional image is crucial, yet many businesses struggle to get it right. A well-known example comes from a local café owner who went viral not for their coffee, but for a heartfelt video featuring their barista team celebrating a regular customer's milestone birthday. The video wasn't polished or overproduced, but it struck a chord because it showcased real people, genuine emotions, and the spirit of the café. This moment of authenticity, shared widely on social media, exemplifies the power of balancing humanity with professionalism.

To start, avoid the temptation to make your content feel overly staged. **Highly polished content often risks feeling distant, while candid, relatable posts foster a stronger connection with your audience.** For example, instead of hiring models for your restaurant's social media, consider featuring your actual staff preparing dishes or serving customers. Authentic moments resonate more deeply because they reflect the true character of your brand. A short clip of your chef sharing a cooking tip or a photo of your team sharing a laugh after a busy shift adds personality that polished ads often lack.

At the same time, professionalism ensures that your brand remains credible and reliable. **This means maintaining high visual standards without sacrificing warmth or relatability.** Use quality lighting and sound in your videos and ensure that text in captions is free from errors. Even in informal posts, avoid language that might appear overly casual or out of sync with your brand's values. Striking this balance demonstrates respect for your audience while preserving a professional reputation.

A vital element of this strategy is showcasing the

people behind your brand. **Introducing your team not only humanizes your business but also fosters a sense of community among your audience.** A short feature on your bartender's favorite cocktail recipe or a behind-the-scenes look at how your team prepares for a busy night helps customers see the effort and care that goes into their experience. These glimpses into daily operations make your brand more relatable while reinforcing the professionalism of your work.

Integrating stories about your customers can also deepen the connection. **Highlighting loyal patrons, sharing their testimonials, or celebrating their special moments can make your content both authentic and engaging.** If a family chooses your restaurant for a major celebration, share their story with their permission. These moments create a narrative that other customers can see themselves in, strengthening their emotional connection to your brand.

Finally, consistency is key to balancing authenticity and professionalism. **Ensure that your tone, style, and visual identity remain cohesive across all platforms.** Whether you're sharing a playful video of a kitchen mishap or a formal announcement about new menu items, every piece of content should align with the values and image you want to project. Professionalism isn't about being perfect; it's about being intentional and thoughtful in how you represent your brand while staying true to its core.

In a world where audiences are increasingly skeptical of overly curated content, embracing authenticity while maintaining a polished presence is more important than ever. By showing your human side, telling genuine stories, and presenting them with care, your brand can build lasting trust and meaningful connections.

CHAPTER 4
GROWING YOUR AUDIENCE ORGANICALLY
BUILD A LOYAL FOLLOWING WITHOUT SPENDING A FORTUNE

What's the secret to growing an audience that genuinely cares about your business without draining your budget? The answer lies in crafting meaningful connections. Businesses often assume they need a hefty advertising budget to attract followers, but building an organic audience is about more than spending money—it's about showing up consistently, engaging authentically, and adding real value to people's lives.

Attracting a loyal following starts with understanding the community you want to create. When people follow a business online, they're not just looking for updates—they're seeking a sense of belonging, an experience, or something that aligns with their values. Whether it's a local bakery sharing heartfelt stories of regular customers or a small boutique giving behind-the-scenes looks at new arrivals, successful businesses find ways to bring their followers into their world. **The** key is to think less about selling and more about building relationships.

Engagement plays an equally important role in growth. Posting content is only one part of the equation; how you interact with your audience can make a bigger difference. **Responding to comments, asking for opinions, or sparking conversations in your posts transforms followers into active participants.** This interaction signals to your audience that their voice matters, which keeps them coming back and encourages them to share your content with others. Platforms reward this kind of activity, too, pushing engaging accounts to broader audiences.

Another piece of the puzzle is showcasing what makes your business unique. Authentic storytelling, whether it's a quick video about your daily operations or a post celebrating a milestone, helps potential followers see why your page is worth their time. **When your content feels genuine and distinct, people are more likely to follow and recommend you to others.** This also ensures that you're attracting the right audience—those who are likely to become long-term supporters, not just casual observers.

Organic growth may take more time and effort than paid promotions, but its rewards run deeper. By focusing on attracting followers who are truly invested in what you do, you create a base of loyal advocates who will amplify your reach without you needing to ask. As the upcoming sections will explore, there are specific strategies to make this approach both effective and manageable, from creating shareable content to leveraging local connections. Together, these tactics form the foundation of growing your audience organically in a way that lasts.

Engaging with Your Audience Daily

Every brand has a story, but the ones that thrive tell theirs through meaningful conversations. Consider the story of a local café owner who took the time to personally respond to every Instagram comment and message, even when it meant staying up late. Within months, the café's followers doubled, and its loyal customers began referring to it as "their" coffee shop. The owner wasn't just running a business; they were creating a relationship, and their audience responded by becoming not just patrons but advocates. This simple act of engagement transformed a modest online presence into a thriving digital community.

Engaging with your audience daily isn't just a box to check—it's the digital handshake that makes followers feel valued. When you promptly respond to comments and messages, you're doing more than acknowledging someone's words; you're demonstrating that their voice matters. **Timely replies build trust and encourage others to interact more openly, creating a ripple effect that strengthens your presence.** This approach isn't limited to praise; handling questions or addressing concerns with care can also turn potential detractors into loyal supporters.

Beyond responses, initiating conversations is a powerful way to deepen connections. **Ask open-ended questions in your posts or stories, sparking discussions that invite your audience to participate.** People are naturally drawn to brands that show curiosity about their opinions, whether it's about their favorite menu item or suggestions for future events. These interactions signal that your brand is listening, transforming casual followers into engaged contributors to your content.

Another effective strategy is to celebrate those who support your business. Highlighting loyal customers through shout-outs, reposting their photos with credit, or thanking them publicly fosters a sense of community. **This not only strengthens relationships with existing customers but also signals to potential followers that your brand values people over transactions.** Research has shown that audiences are more likely to engage with brands they perceive as authentic and caring, which further underscores the importance of genuine appreciation.

Gary Vaynerchuk's insights in *Crushing It!* reinforce this principle: daily engagement isn't just a task—it's an opportunity. He argues that consistent, thoughtful interactions build the kind of loyalty that can't be bought with ads. **When you treat every comment, tag, or message as a chance to create a connection, you're laying the foundation for long-term growth.** This mindset shifts engagement from a chore to a strategy, one that pays dividends in loyalty and organic visibility.

In the fast-moving world of social media, where algorithms reward authentic interaction, your willingness to invest time in engagement sets you apart. It humanizes your brand, creates advocates, and establishes a dialogue that extends beyond likes and shares. As we explore the deeper layers of audience-building strategies, remember that each interaction is an opportunity to build a bridge. With the right approach, these small moments can add up to a thriving, loyal community.

Collaborating with Local Influencers

Why do some local businesses seem to explode in popularity overnight while others struggle to get noticed? Often, the answer lies in the power of influencer collaborations. When a neighborhood restaurant teamed up with a well-known food blogger who lived just a few blocks away, they saw a 30% increase in foot traffic within two weeks. This wasn't the result of flashy ads or expensive campaigns—it was a carefully planned partnership that aligned their menu with the influencer's authentic style.

Collaborating with local influencers can transform your brand's visibility, but success depends on choosing the right partners. **Micro-influencers—those with 1,000 to 50,000 followers—often bring higher engagement**

rates than large-scale celebrities. According to a 2022 study by Influencer Marketing Hub, micro-influencers have an average engagement rate of 3.86%, compared to just 1.21% for mega-influencers. These individuals are trusted by their communities and can deliver your message in a way that feels genuine, making them ideal partners for local campaigns.

Finding these influencers requires more than a quick internet search. **Use tools like Instagram's search feature or influencer marketing platforms to locate accounts that align with your values and appeal to your audience.** For example, if your brand emphasizes sustainability, look for influencers who post about eco-friendly dining or showcase responsible lifestyle choices. Always review their past content to ensure their tone, audience, and aesthetics match your goals.

Once you've identified a potential collaborator, approach them with a clear value exchange. Instead of offering only cash, consider providing free meals, exclusive access to events, or behind-the-scenes experiences that they can share with their followers. **This type of arrangement feels less transactional and fosters authenticity in their posts.** Research published in the *Journal of Consumer Psychology* highlights that audiences are more likely to trust and engage with influencer content when it appears to come from personal enthusiasm rather than a paid advertisement.

Measuring the success of these campaigns is essential to refine your strategy. **Track metrics such as** referral traffic, social media mentions, and post engagement to evaluate the impact of an influencer's efforts. Use unique discount codes or custom URLs to tie specific sales directly to a campaign. By analyzing these results, you can determine which influencers resonate most with your audience and optimize future partnerships.

Authenticity remains the cornerstone of successful collaborations. Influencers who genuinely appreciate your product will naturally convey that enthusiasm to their followers. These partnerships aren't just about advertising—they're about creating real connections between your brand and the community. When done thoughtfully, they become a powerful tool for building trust, generating buzz, and driving sustained growth.

Hosting Social Media Giveaways

"A well-crafted giveaway can generate as much excitement as a grand opening," a small bakery owner once said after their follower count doubled in less than a month. They had offered a year's worth of free croissants to one lucky participant, but the real prize was the thousands of new followers and customers who discovered their shop through the contest. Stories like this show that a smartly planned giveaway can do more than bring temporary attention—it can build a lasting connection with your audience.

The foundation of a successful giveaway is choosing

a prize that is both enticing and relevant to your brand. **An ideal prize is something that showcases what makes your business unique, whether it's a signature product, exclusive experience, or limited-edition item.** For a coffee shop, this might be a "coffee for a month" deal. A spa might offer a complimentary deluxe package. The more tailored the prize is to your offerings, the more likely you are to attract participants who are genuinely interested in your brand rather than casual contest-seekers.

Equally important is structuring the rules to serve your business goals while remaining compliant with platform guidelines. **On Instagram and Facebook, clear requirements like "follow our page, tag a friend, and comment your favorite product" can increase visibility and engagement without violating the rules.** Instagram's promotion policies, for example, require transparency about the fact that the giveaway is not associated with Instagram itself. Ensure your wording is clear, avoids false claims, and protects participant data.

A giveaway also offers an excellent chance to grow your email and text lists. **To maximize this opportunity, encourage participants to sign up through a landing page that collects their contact information.** Tools like Mailchimp or Constant Contact allow you to integrate these sign-ups directly into your marketing platform. Combining email and text opt-ins with your giveaway not only expands your audience but also creates future opportunities to reach them with targeted offers.

Timing and promotion are also crucial to your giveaway's success. **The ideal giveaway runs long enough to gain traction—typically five to seven days—but not so long that interest wanes.** Promote the event across all your channels, including your website, social media platforms, and even in-store signage. Collaborate with influencers or loyal customers to amplify your reach by asking them to share the giveaway with their followers. If possible, consider aligning the contest with a seasonal theme, holiday, or milestone that adds excitement.

After the giveaway ends, its impact doesn't stop. **Follow up with all participants, not just the winner, to keep the momentum going.** Send a thank-you email with a small reward, such as a discount code or exclusive offer, as a token of appreciation. This follow-up not only fosters goodwill but also encourages continued engagement and purchases.

Hosting a giveaway is about more than gaining a quick spike in likes and comments. When executed with thoughtfulness and strategy, it becomes a powerful tool to strengthen your connection with existing followers while drawing in new ones. By focusing on prizes that reflect your brand, adhering to rules, and leveraging the event to grow your contact lists, you can transform a simple contest into a long-term win for your business.

Joining Trending Conversations

"Joining a trend is like grabbing the mic at a crowded

karaoke bar," a small café owner once joked after their rendition of a viral coffee recipe brought thousands of new followers to their social media page. The light-hearted comment highlights a key point: participating in trending conversations gives your brand a stage in front of an engaged and curious audience. When done right, it's not just about visibility—it's about creating memorable and meaningful connections.

One of the most effective ways to enter trending conversations is by identifying viral challenges or hashtags that align with your brand's personality. **Look for trends that are already gaining traction within your industry or that can be easily adapted to showcase your unique offerings.** For example, if a popular hashtag is about comfort food, a pizza shop might post a video of their team crafting a giant, over-the-top pepperoni pie. The key is to ensure your contribution feels authentic rather than forced.

Tailoring a trend to fit your voice is essential for maintaining credibility. **Your audience is more likely to engage with content that reflects your genuine personality rather than an awkward attempt to ride a viral wave.** If your restaurant is known for its friendly, quirky vibe, your posts can incorporate humor or unexpected twists. For a fine dining establishment, a more polished approach with stunning visuals might better reflect your brand. By staying true to your identity, you build trust while participating in wider conversations.

Avoiding controversy is equally important. While

trending topics often attract massive attention, not every trend is worth joining. **Steer clear of polarizing or divisive subjects that could alienate your audience or bring negative publicity.** Instead, focus on positive, inclusive trends that resonate broadly. For instance, a bakery might join a seasonal trend, like posting creative takes on pumpkin-flavored treats in October, rather than wading into debates that could overshadow the message.

Tracking the impact of your participation in trends is another critical step. **Measure engagement metrics like likes, shares, comments, and new followers to understand how well your content resonated with your audience.** Use tools like Instagram Insights or TikTok Analytics to track these numbers. Observing which trends brought the most attention can help refine your future strategy, allowing you to focus on conversations that align with your goals.

Joining trending conversations isn't about being trendy for its own sake—it's about using those moments to amplify your voice and connect with people in a way that feels natural. By aligning with the right trends, adapting them to your unique style, and avoiding missteps, your participation can go beyond fleeting engagement to foster a deeper and lasting connection with your audience.

CHAPTER 5
RUNNING PAID SOCIAL MEDIA CAMPAIGNS

MAXIMIZE ROI WITH TARGETED ADS THAT DRIVE RESERVATIONS

Imagine owning a restaurant where every table is filled because people keep discovering your ad on their social feeds. Paid social media campaigns have made this a reality for countless businesses, turning once-empty dining rooms into bustling hubs of activity. At their core, these campaigns are about precision—targeting the right people with messages that inspire action, whether it's making a reservation, visiting your website, or exploring your menu. Unlike traditional advertising, they allow you to reach specific audiences in real time, optimizing every dollar spent for maximum impact.

The key to running successful campaigns lies in understanding the balance between creativity and strategy. **Compelling visuals and clear messaging draw people in, but it's the strategic use of targeting tools that ensures your ads reach the right eyes.** Social media platforms like Facebook, Instagram, and TikTok offer advanced options to define your audience based on location, age, interests, and even their dining habits. This means your restaurant doesn't just advertise—it connects with people already looking for the experiences you offer.

Budgeting for paid ads might seem daunting at first, but it's more approachable than many realize. Platforms are designed to accommodate campaigns of all sizes, letting you test small-scale efforts before committing to a larger spend. **The flexibility of these tools allows you to experiment, learn, and refine your approach to make sure your investment pays off.** With detailed analytics, you can measure how well your ads perform, adjusting your strategy to focus on what works best.

The value of these campaigns goes beyond immediate clicks and bookings. **They help build long-term relationships by keeping your restaurant top of mind.** Even when someone doesn't act on an ad right away, repeated exposure can turn curiosity into loyalty over time. By using retargeting, you can re-engage potential customers who showed interest in your offerings but didn't take the next step, gently guiding them back to your table.

Running paid campaigns requires more than just setting up an ad and hoping for results—it demands a thoughtful approach. Every element, from the imagery to the call-to-action, needs to align with your brand's voice and goals. By focusing on what makes your restaurant unique and learning to leverage social media's robust advertising tools, you can create campaigns that don't just attract attention but convert it into real-world results. This chapter will explore the strategies, tools, and insights needed to make paid social media campaigns a powerful part of your marketing playbook.

Understanding Paid Social Advertising Basics

A small café in Austin decided to boost a single Instagram post about their seasonal lattes, spending just $50 to experiment. Within days, the post had reached thousands of potential customers, doubling their usual engagement and bringing in dozens of new faces eager to try the promoted drinks. This is the power of understanding the basics of paid social advertising: small actions, when done strategically, can yield significant results.

At the heart of paid social lies the distinction between **boosted posts** and **ad campaigns**. Boosted posts are simple promotions of content that already exists on your social media page. They are designed to increase visibility among a broader audience without requiring extensive setup. In contrast, ad campaigns involve a deeper level of customization, allowing businesses to create ads tailored to specific objectives like driving traffic to a website, generating sales, or encouraging app downloads. **Boosted posts are great for expanding brand awareness quickly, while ad campaigns offer precise targeting and measurable outcomes for more complex goals.** Knowing when to use each is crucial for maximizing the impact of your advertising budget.

Choosing the right objective for an ad campaign often determines its success. Most platforms like Facebook, Instagram, and TikTok let you define objectives such as clicks, views, or sales. **If your goal is to drive reservations, prioritize conversions or click-based objectives that lead users to your booking page.** For building awareness, focus on reach or engagement objectives to spread your message broadly. Selecting the correct goal ensures your campaign aligns with what you want to achieve, avoiding wasted effort and resources.

Starting small is a wise approach for businesses new to paid advertising. Testing campaigns with modest budgets—say $20 to $100—helps identify what works before committing more resources. This method minimizes risk while providing valuable data on audience preferences and content effectiveness. **By analyzing early results, such as which images or headlines generate the most clicks, you can refine future campaigns and allocate your budget where it delivers the highest return.**

Platforms like Meta Ads Manager or TikTok Ads

make it simple to experiment and learn, offering real-time feedback on performance. They break down metrics like cost per click (CPC), impressions, and conversions, helping you understand how your ads resonate with your audience. **This transparency allows you to adapt quickly, shifting strategies to capitalize on opportunities or address underperforming campaigns.** Treat these tools as both a guide and a teacher, as they provide insights that improve your skills over time.

Investing time in mastering these basics creates a foundation for long-term success. Whether you're boosting posts to engage your local community or running targeted campaigns aimed at specific demographics, understanding the principles of paid advertising gives you control over your brand's visibility. The café in Austin didn't just increase foot traffic—they learned how to target seasonal drink lovers, a valuable insight they applied to future campaigns with even greater results. Knowing the difference between tactics, setting clear objectives, and starting with small steps leads to a smarter, more effective strategy for growth.

Targeting the Right Audience

Can you imagine creating an ad that feels like it was designed specifically for you? That's the kind of connection effective audience targeting can achieve. By using data about demographics, interests, and behaviors, businesses have the power to speak directly to the people most likely to engage, buy, or visit. In fact, targeted ads are 2.5 times more effective than non-targeted ones, according to a study by WordStream. Understanding how to refine and test your audience is the difference between a campaign that thrives and one that falls flat.

Audience targeting begins with demographics—basic characteristics like age, gender, location, and income level. These details set the stage for understanding who your ideal customer is. **If you're running a family-friendly restaurant, your focus might be on parents aged 25 to 40 in your city.** For a boutique wine bar, you may look at professionals aged 30 and older with a higher income range. The key is to align your ad content with the audience's needs, ensuring every dollar spent on advertising is aimed at the right people.

Interests and behaviors add a deeper layer of precision. Platforms like Meta and TikTok track users' activities, from pages they follow to purchases they've made. This wealth of data allows you to refine your targeting to reach those already inclined to engage with businesses like yours. **For example, a local coffee shop might target users who follow wellness pages or frequently engage with morning routine content.** This approach ensures your ads appear in front of people who are most likely to care about what you offer.

Retargeting is another essential component of audience targeting. This involves reaching out to people who have already interacted with your business—those who visited your website, clicked on a previous ad, or joined your email list. Retargeting works because these individuals are already familiar with your brand and may need just a nudge to take the next step. **A restaurant could retarget visitors who browsed the menu page without making a reservation, offering them a discount code or a reminder about an upcoming special event.** This strategy turns passive interest into active engagement.

Testing different audience groups is critical for understanding what works. Running multiple ad sets targeted at distinct audiences allows you to compare performance and adjust your strategy. **You might discover that younger audiences respond better to video ads, while older demographics engage more with carousel posts showcasing your offerings.** Testing provides clarity on which segments of your audience deliver the highest return on investment, so you can scale those efforts while refining or discarding others.

The beauty of modern advertising platforms lies in their ability to provide detailed insights into audience behavior. Metrics like click-through rates, conversions, and cost per result allow you to see exactly how your campaigns are performing with different groups. **If an ad targeting young professionals achieves lower engagement than expected, you can tweak the messaging or switch the focus to another group entirely.** This level of control ensures your campaigns are always moving closer to success.

By understanding your audience on a granular level, you can create ads that feel relevant and personal. From demographic targeting to retargeting and testing, each step builds on the last to refine your message and maximize your impact. When done well, audience targeting doesn't just bring in more customers; it strengthens the relationship between your brand and the community it serves. The goal isn't just to sell—it's to connect.

Designing Ads That Convert

"Great ads don't just sell products; they tell stories that spark action," said David Ogilvy, often referred to as the father of modern advertising. This truth rings especially loud in the digital age, where attention spans are short, and competition is fierce. The success of your ad depends on its ability to stop someone mid-scroll, make them pause, and compel them to engage. Designing ads that convert is as much about art as it is about science. Every element—the headline, visuals, and format—plays a critical role in influencing behavior.

A headline is the first point of contact between your ad and its audience. **It should be sharp, clear, and instantly relevant to the viewer's needs or desires.** Imagine a restaurant advertising a special brunch menu. A headline like "Wake Up to the Best Pancakes in Town!" is more engaging than a generic "Try Our Brunch Specials." Effective headlines are also concise—research shows that ads with shorter, to-the-point text perform better on platforms like Facebook and Instagram. Words like "exclusive," "limited," and "only today" can create urgency, encouraging immediate action.

Equally important are the visuals. High-quality images or videos draw the eye and communicate value faster than words alone. **The visuals should align with your brand's identity and evoke an emotional response.** For a fine dining restaurant, a close-up shot of a perfectly plated dish with warm lighting might create a sense of luxury. In contrast, a casual eatery might use dynamic, colorful images of people enjoying food together to convey a sense of fun and community. Consistency is key—your visuals should feel like an extension of your brand, reinforcing its personality and promise.

Experimenting with different ad formats is crucial for finding what resonates most with your audience. Platforms like Facebook and Instagram offer a range of options, from carousel ads to videos to stories. **Carousel ads are particularly effective for showcasing multiple products or menu items.** Each slide can feature a different dish, drink, or customer review, allowing viewers to explore without leaving the ad. Videos, on the other hand, are powerful storytelling tools. A short, engaging clip showing the preparation of a signature dish or behind-the-scenes moments in the kitchen can foster a deeper connection with potential customers. Stories, with their ephemeral nature, work well for promoting time-sensitive offers, like happy hour deals or pop-up events.

Testing is the secret ingredient to creating ads that consistently perform. By running multiple versions of an ad with slight variations—such as different headlines, images, or formats—you can determine what captures attention and drives results. **For example, a restaurant might test two ads: one with a vibrant image of a dish and another with a video of a chef preparing it.** Analyzing the click-through and conversion rates of each helps you refine future campaigns. A/B testing like this ensures you're not just guessing but using real data to guide your decisions.

The power of designing ads that convert lies in understanding your audience's preferences and crafting every element of the ad to meet those expectations. From the wording of a headline to the choice of a photo or video, every detail contributes to whether someone scrolls past or stops to engage. A well-designed ad doesn't just attract attention—it inspires action, creating a connection that leads to reservations, visits, and lasting loyalty.

Measuring and Optimizing Campaigns

In the world of digital advertising, where every click, impression, and conversion is tracked, success depends on your ability to interpret and act on this data. Campaigns are not static; they're living strategies that evolve based on performance. Knowing how to measure results effectively and make informed adjustments separates campaigns that deliver from those that waste budgets.

The foundation of optimization begins with tracking the right metrics. Analytics tools provided by platforms like Facebook Ads Manager and Google Ads give detailed insights into ad performance. **Metrics such as click-through rates (CTR), cost-per-click (CPC), and conversion rates reveal how well your ad resonates with the audience and drives the intended action.** For example, a high CTR paired with a low conversion rate could indicate that the ad is appealing but the landing page is not compelling enough. On the other hand, a low CTR might mean the ad itself isn't engaging.

Identifying underperforming ads is not about assigning blame but uncovering opportunities for improvement. **A restaurant promoting a special event might notice that video ads outperform static images.** In this case, shifting more resources to video formats can amplify engagement. Similarly, if an ad targeting young professionals isn't generating interest, refining the audience's age range or tweaking the language to better match their preferences can lead to better results. Adjustments should always be data-driven, with clear reasons for every change.

Scaling successful campaigns is where optimization turns into growth. When an ad performs well, increasing its budget or expanding its reach can maximize impact. **For instance, if a limited-time offer ad is driving significant sales in one region, consider expanding the same ad to neighboring areas or targeting a broader demographic.** However, scaling should be gradual and monitored closely to ensure returns remain consistent. Sudden increases in budget can sometimes lead to diminishing returns, making careful observation crucial.

A/B testing remains one of the most effective tools for continuous improvement. By running variations of an ad with small changes—like adjusting headlines, visuals, or calls to action—you can pinpoint what resonates most with your audience. **For example, testing two versions of an ad promoting a new menu item—one highlighting affordability and the other focusing on exclusivity—can reveal which message is more effective.** This iterative approach ensures that campaigns evolve in response to audience behavior, becoming more efficient over time.

The optimization process doesn't stop after the campaign ends. Post-campaign analysis provides valuable lessons for future efforts. By reviewing key metrics and identifying what worked and what didn't, you can refine your strategies and set benchmarks for upcoming campaigns. **This reflection ensures that every campaign builds on the success and learnings of the previous one, creating a cycle of improvement.**

Measuring and optimizing campaigns is about more than just numbers; it's about understanding your audience, refining your message, and adapting to what works. The ability to listen to the data and respond thoughtfully transforms advertising from a cost into an investment, ensuring that every dollar spent brings your brand closer to its goals.

CHAPTER 6
MANAGING YOUR RESTAURANT'S ONLINE REPUTATION

TURN SOCIAL MEDIA FEEDBACK INTO POSITIVE RELATIONSHIPS

What's the first thing customers do after a memorable dining experience—good or bad? They talk about it, often online. Whether through a glowing review on Google, a comment on Instagram, or a frustrated tweet, your restaurant's reputation increasingly lives in the digital world. Managing that reputation is no longer optional; it's an essential part of running a successful business. A single comment has the power to draw in new guests or send them running to your competitors.

Understanding how to navigate online feedback is about more than damage control. **It's about transforming customer interactions into opportunities for connection, growth, and trust.** Positive reviews can become marketing gold, amplifying your brand's appeal. Meanwhile, tactfully handled negative feedback shows your audience that you value transparency and customer satisfaction, building a deeper sense of loyalty.

In a time when 77% of diners say they rely on online reviews before choosing where to eat (BrightLocal, 2023), your response strategy directly impacts your bottom line.

Responding to feedback effectively requires a blend of timeliness, empathy, and strategic thinking. **A restaurant owner who thoughtfully addresses customer concerns—not with defensiveness, but with genuine care—can turn a disappointed diner into a devoted fan.** For instance, a critical review about long wait times might be a chance to highlight changes you've implemented, like a new reservation system or updated staffing. Public responses show all potential customers that you take feedback seriously, making your restaurant more approachable and trustworthy.

It's also essential to recognize that managing your online presence isn't just reactive. Proactively asking for feedback creates a continuous loop of improvement while boosting your online reputation. Encouraging satisfied customers to share their experiences increases the volume of positive content about your brand, effectively burying occasional negative remarks in a sea of praise. Platforms like Yelp, Google, and Facebook reward businesses with more reviews by improving their search visibility, helping you reach new audiences organically.

A strong reputation doesn't happen by chance. It's built through consistency, care, and a willingness to engage with your audience, even when the feedback stings. **Your ability to manage reviews and social interactions shapes how customers see you, well before they step through your doors.**

Responding to Comments and Reviews

A frustrated customer recently shared a one-star review about a restaurant's slow service during a busy Friday night. The comment described the long wait and how it overshadowed the otherwise delicious meal. Within hours, the restaurant manager responded with an apology, acknowledged the delay, and assured the reviewer of ongoing efforts to improve staffing during peak times. To the surprise of many, the reviewer updated their rating to three stars, adding, "They genuinely care about their customers." This story underscores the value of responding thoughtfully to feedback, even when it's critical.

Acknowledging comments and reviews—both good and bad—allows businesses to shape how they are perceived. **When customers take the time to share their thoughts, responding shows that you are listening and value their opinions.** Positive comments provide an opportunity to reinforce loyalty by thanking customers for their support. A simple acknowledgment like "We're thrilled you enjoyed the experience—thank you for sharing!" not only deepens the relationship with that customer but also sends a welcoming message to others reading the exchange.

Handling negative feedback requires a different level of care. **Responding with empathy and professionalism can turn a potentially damaging comment into an opportunity for improvement.** Start by expressing understanding of the customer's frustration, then take responsibility if appropriate, and explain any steps you are taking to resolve the issue. For instance, a review about incorrect orders might prompt a response like, "We're sorry to hear about the mix-up. We've recently introduced a double-check system for orders, and we'd love to invite you back to experience the changes." This not only addresses the specific concern but demonstrates a proactive approach to customer satisfaction.

Social media expands the conversation beyond traditional review platforms, turning every comment into an opportunity for interaction. **When customers tag your restaurant in posts or comment on your updates, replying quickly keeps the dialogue alive and shows engagement.** Use this as a chance to build rapport, whether by sharing excitement about their visit or humorously engaging with their post. Restaurants that use social platforms as an extension of their customer service create a sense of accessibility that resonates with today's digital-savvy diners.

Beyond individual interactions, tracking patterns in feedback reveals areas needing improvement. A recurring theme in comments, like complaints about wait times or noise levels, might highlight operational inefficiencies to address. By treating comments and reviews as actionable data, businesses can adapt and grow. It's not about perfection but progress—and ensuring every customer feels heard along the way.

Pro Tip: Every restaurant should consider posting a playful, tongue-in-cheek 1-star review that cleverly highlights what makes the restaurant extraordinary. For instance, "Awful experience—now I can't eat pizza anywhere else because nothing compares. The crust was too perfectly crispy, the sauce was too rich, and the staff was annoyingly friendly. Thanks for ruining every other pizza place for me!" This tactic is particularly effective because many people start by reading the negative reviews to judge an establishment. A cleverly crafted "negative" review that's actually a humble brag will catch their attention, create intrigue, and turn what could be skepticism into curiosity or even excitement about your restaurant.

Proactively Encouraging Positive Reviews

What motivates a customer to leave a glowing review after a meal? Studies show that convenience and a sense of appreciation play significant roles. According to a survey by BrightLocal, 87% of consumers read online reviews for local businesses, but only a fraction take the time to write one. This highlights an important reality: creating an environment where leaving feedback is both simple and rewarding is key to encouraging positive reviews.

Making the review process effortless starts with technology. **Using QR codes strategically placed on menus, receipts, or even table tents can guide customers directly to your review platform.** These codes eliminate barriers like searching for the business online, providing a direct path for immediate feedback. For example, a restaurant that places a QR code on its receipt, accompanied by a friendly note such as "We value your thoughts," can transform a casual diner into an active advocate.

Recognizing and rewarding detailed feedback enhances the likelihood of consistent positive reviews. **Incentives like discounts, loyalty points, or entry into a prize draw can encourage customers to share their experiences in depth.** Rewards should be meaningful but tied to authentic engagement rather than simply offering generic perks. A customer who feels their voice is heard and appreciated is more likely to leave thoughtful feedback, providing valuable insights for the business while boosting its online reputation.

Amplifying the impact of positive reviews requires strategic sharing. **When customers see their glowing feedback featured on your social media or website, it not only builds their loyalty but also strengthens trust among potential diners.** By showcasing authentic customer stories—whether it's a tweet praising your signature dish or a Facebook review highlighting exceptional service—you signal to your audience that you prioritize customer satisfaction. Brittany Hennessy, in her book *Influencer*, emphasizes the importance of authenticity in building trust. She notes that genuine testimonials resonate more deeply than polished advertisements, making real reviews a powerful marketing tool.

Proactively managing reviews isn't just about collecting positive feedback; it's about fostering a culture of trust and connection. When customers feel that their opinions genuinely matter, they become more than patrons—they become advocates who champion your business to their peers. This cycle of engagement and recognition not only strengthens your reputation but creates a foundation for lasting loyalty.

Handling Online Criticism with Grace

"When critics don't find you, they invent you," wrote Oscar Wilde, highlighting the inevitability of facing criticism, particularly in the public sphere. For restaurants, this truth plays out in the digital realm, where every comment, review, and rating has the potential to shape reputation and revenue. The way criticism is addressed often matters more than the critique itself, making grace and strategy essential tools in handling online feedback.

One common misstep is responding defensively to negative reviews, which can amplify tension and turn small grievances into public spectacles. Instead, **acknowledging the reviewer's concerns with empathy** can diffuse anger and signal to potential customers that the restaurant values feedback. A response like, "We're sorry to hear about your experience; this doesn't meet the standard we aim for, and we'd like to make it right," transforms a complaint into an opportunity to show integrity. This approach not only reassures the reviewer but also sends a message to others reading the exchange that the business is proactive and customer-focused.

Sometimes, addressing criticism publicly isn't enough. **Taking sensitive conversations offline is crucial when the issue is too complex for a comment thread.** Inviting the customer to discuss the matter privately via email or phone can de-escalate emotions and prevent further misunderstandings. For example, if a diner complains about an allergen-related mishap, replying publicly with an apology and offering a direct line to resolve the issue privately shows accountability without airing every detail to the internet. This tactic also ensures the restaurant maintains control over the narrative while preserving the customer's dignity.

Criticism, when constructive, offers a rare gift: insight into areas for improvement. **Analyzing recurring themes in negative reviews can reveal patterns that might otherwise go unnoticed.** If multiple reviews mention long wait times or inconsistencies in service, it signals an operational issue that requires attention. Implementing changes based on this feedback, such as refining scheduling processes or retraining staff, not only improves the customer experience but also turns detractors into advocates. Following up with reviewers to let them know their concerns were addressed can leave a lasting positive impression.

Learning to handle criticism with grace requires seeing each piece of feedback as an opportunity rather than an attack. By staying composed, listening carefully, and taking meaningful action, restaurants can turn even the harshest critiques into stepping stones toward a stronger reputation. These efforts demonstrate not just the quality of the food or service but the quality of character behind the brand.

Monitoring Your Brand Online

"Reputation is an idle and most false imposition; oft got without merit, and lost without deserving," wrote William Shakespeare. Today, this sentiment resonates profoundly in the digital landscape, where a single tweet or trending hashtag can make or break perceptions of a brand. For restaurants and businesses, monitoring how they are spoken about online isn't just a task; it's a critical aspect of safeguarding their reputation.

Tracking mentions and hashtags is where this effort begins. Tools like Google Alerts, Hootsuite, and Brand24 allow businesses to monitor social media and other digital platforms for mentions of their name or relevant keywords. **This constant awareness ensures that no**

significant conversation about your brand goes unnoticed, whether it's a glowing review, a viral complaint, or an emerging trend. By setting up alerts for key phrases, like your restaurant's name paired with "complaint" or "review," you can respond swiftly and show attentiveness in real-time.

Sometimes, monitoring goes beyond simple mentions to combat brand misrepresentation. Fake accounts or misleading claims about a business can spread quickly and harm trust. **When faced with misrepresentation or spam, swift action is key**. Reporting such posts to the platform and clarifying facts publicly ensures your audience receives accurate information. For example, if a viral claim suggests your menu contains allergens it doesn't, a prompt, factual response can prevent panic and demonstrate accountability.

Staying aware of broader trends is equally essential. Cultural shifts, new technology, and changing customer preferences can all influence how your brand is perceived. **Trends can also act as signals, offering insight into what customers care about most at a given time**. For instance, if discussions around sustainability surge, highlighting eco-friendly practices in your business can align you with customer values. Monitoring these shifts keeps your brand agile and relevant in an ever-evolving marketplace.

Proactive monitoring allows businesses to stay informed, address issues quickly, and adapt to changing landscapes. By remaining alert and responsive, you ensure that your brand isn't just reacting to conversations but actively shaping them. This vigilance builds trust, reinforces credibility, and strengthens relationships with customers who value transparency and engagement.

CHAPTER 7
SUSTAINING LONG-TERM SOCIAL MEDIA SUCCESS
KEEP YOUR RESTAURANT RELEVANT IN AN EVER-CHANGING DIGITAL WORLD

How does a restaurant stay relevant when social media trends change faster than the daily specials? The world of digital communication is in constant motion, with algorithms evolving, platforms introducing new features, and customer expectations shifting. For restaurants, maintaining a long-term presence on social media requires more than just regular posting; it demands adaptability, strategic thinking, and a deep understanding of your audience.

Consistency is at the heart of sustaining success. Customers trust brands that show up often and align with their expectations. This doesn't mean posting for the sake of posting; it's about delivering value—whether that's through enticing food photos, engaging stories, or genuine responses to questions and comments. By staying consistent, you remind your audience of the experience your restaurant offers, keeping you top of mind when they're deciding where to dine.

Adapting to trends is equally important. Social media users are quick to embrace new formats like short videos or interactive posts, and restaurants that hesitate to adopt these risk feeling outdated. Being adaptable doesn't mean abandoning your brand's identity. Instead, it's about finding ways to integrate new ideas while staying true to your voice. For example, if your restaurant is known for its family-friendly atmosphere, a well-timed video showcasing a family enjoying their favorite dish can resonate deeply without straying from your core message.

Engaging your audience requires forward-thinking strategies that also prepare for changes in how platforms operate. As algorithms prioritize different types of content, your approach to reach customers must evolve. Understanding data from past posts—such as which times of day drive the most engagement or which types of content earn the most shares—allows you to refine your tactics over time. Long-term success isn't about luck; it's about tracking patterns and using that knowledge to improve.

Staying relevant on social media involves balancing consistency and innovation, knowing when to rely on proven methods and when to try something new. By investing in this balance, you create a digital presence that isn't just reactive but proactive, preparing your restaurant to thrive no matter how the online landscape shifts.

Evolving Your Strategy Over Time

Social media strategies are rarely static. When Instagram rolled out Reels in 2020 to compete with TikTok, brands that embraced the feature quickly saw an increase in visibility and engagement. Restaurants, particularly those showcasing vibrant dishes or behind-the-scenes moments, found their content reaching audiences far beyond their immediate followers. This shift wasn't about simply uploading videos; it was about recognizing the potential of a new format and adapting to it before competitors could catch up. Success in digital marketing often hinges on a willingness to pivot and experiment when platforms change the rules of engagement.

Understanding platform updates is not just a technical necessity but a strategic advantage. Algorithms dictate what users see and engage with, and those algorithms change regularly. For example, Facebook's algorithm now prioritizes meaningful interactions, which means a post that sparks conversation can outperform one with a high number of likes. Restaurants can leverage this by crafting posts that ask questions or encourage patrons to share their experiences. Being proactive and staying informed allows businesses to anticipate these shifts rather than reacting to them after losing visibility.

Experimentation with new formats is equally important. Social media trends move fast, and what worked last year might feel outdated today. Live video, AR filters, interactive polls, and ephemeral content like Instagram Stories are all examples of features that were once optional but are now expected by many users. A restaurant that tries new approaches, such as live-streaming a cooking class or using polls to let customers vote on a weekly special, stays relevant and engages its audience in fresh ways. Experimentation should be guided by an understanding of your audience's preferences and not driven by trends alone.

Revisiting goals regularly is the final pillar of a strategy that evolves with time. A restaurant's social media objectives may shift as its business grows or its audience changes. Early goals might center on building awareness, but as followers grow, engagement and conversion could become the focus. Tracking metrics like reach, comments, and click-through rates ensures your strategy aligns with your broader business objectives. Without periodic reviews, efforts can stagnate, and opportunities for growth may be missed.

Evolving your strategy is not a luxury but a necessity in a digital landscape that thrives on novelty. Restaurants that adapt to platform updates, explore new features, and refine their goals remain not only visible but also competitive. Flexibility, paired with a deep understanding of your audience, ensures that your social media presence continues to drive results, no matter how the platforms themselves evolve.

Training Your Team to Manage Social Media

Who understands your restaurant better than the people who work there every day? Your team sees the behind-the-scenes magic, knows what dishes customers rave about, and often hears the feedback you may never get firsthand. When empowered and equipped with the right tools, these insights can transform your restaurant's social media presence into an authentic and engaging extension of your brand. But training your team to contribute effectively requires intention, strategy, and clear guidance.

Empowering your staff begins by inviting them into the creative process. Front-of-house servers hear customer reactions to new menu items, bartenders notice which drinks get the most Instagram-worthy nods, and kitchen staff know what ingredients or techniques make dishes stand out. Encouraging team members to share their observations can uncover content ideas that resonate with customers. For example, a chef's tip on how to make the perfect risotto or a server's story about a loyal customer's favorite dish can create engaging posts that bring your brand to life. The key is to ensure staff feel comfortable sharing their ideas without judgment or the pressure of execution, knowing their contributions are valued.

Equipping your team with basic social media training is essential to building confidence and consistency. Tools like Canva for graphic creation or Later for scheduling posts can demystify the process, especially for staff unfamiliar with the technical side of social media. Training doesn't have to be overwhelming. Short sessions on how to capture high-quality photos using a smartphone, write captions that reflect your brand's voice, or engage with comments authentically can make a significant impact. A well-trained team not only strengthens your online presence but also prevents missteps that could arise from unintentional errors.

Delegating roles ensures your posting schedule stays consistent without overwhelming any single person. This involves assigning clear responsibilities, such as designating someone to capture daily photos, another to monitor comments, and perhaps a lead to oversee and approve content before it's posted. Consistency in your posting schedule builds trust with your audience and ensures your brand remains top of mind. It also prevents the chaos of last-minute scrambling for content, which can result in missed opportunities or poorly executed posts.

A collaborative social media strategy transforms your team from passive participants into active ambassadors for your brand. By empowering staff to share ideas, equipping them with tools and training, and delegating roles thoughtfully, your restaurant's social media becomes a dynamic reflection of the people and stories that make your establishment unique. This approach not only lightens the load on management but also strengthens the bond between your team and your audience, fostering a sense of shared purpose that resonates both online and in the dining room.

Leveraging Analytics for Continuous Improvement

"Data beats opinion." This quote, often attributed to Jim Barksdale, highlights a simple truth: informed decisions yield better outcomes. In the fast-paced world of social media, where trends evolve overnight, leveraging analytics is not just helpful—it's essential. Numbers don't lie, and when you learn to interpret them, they can illuminate the path to more effective strategies, deeper connections, and greater success.

Analyzing audience engagement starts with identifying patterns in how your followers interact with your content. Look for trends in the times they are most active, the types of posts that get the highest likes, comments, or shares, and even the ones that seem to fall flat. Platforms like Instagram and Facebook provide detailed insights into these metrics. If a short video of a chef preparing a dish consistently outperforms static images, it's a sign to lean into dynamic content. On the other hand, if polls and questions bring the most comments, it could mean your audience values interaction. Understanding these patterns allows you to refine your approach, delivering content that resonates.

Insights from analytics do more than just shape your content—they also reveal what isn't working. If posts about menu updates consistently have low reach, it may signal a need to experiment with presentation. Perhaps framing updates through storytelling or incorporating video could improve engagement. Data helps remove the guesswork, offering concrete ways to tweak strategies and ensure every post serves a purpose. **By focusing on what performs well and rethinking weaker areas, you continuously fine-tune your approach, optimizing for growth.**

Celebrating wins, no matter how small, keeps your momentum going. Analytics provide measurable proof of success, whether it's a jump in followers, a boost in post shares, or a spike in website visits after a campaign. Acknowledge these milestones within your team. Recognizing what works well also fosters a culture of improvement and encourages creativity in future planning. At the same time, failures are equally valuable when approached with curiosity instead of frustration. If an idea flops, ask why. Did it miss the mark with your audience, or was it posted at the wrong time? Use these moments as learning opportunities rather than setbacks.

Learning to read and act on analytics transforms your social media presence into a well-oiled, ever-improving system. It's not just about tracking numbers; it's about understanding the story they tell. Armed with these insights, you can craft strategies that adapt to changing preferences, highlight your strengths, and evolve with your audience, ensuring your brand stays relevant and impactful.

Building a Social Media Legacy

"Legacy is not what I did for myself. It's what I'm doing for the next generation," said Vitor Belfort, a sentiment that perfectly aligns with the goal of building a lasting social media presence. In the digital age, a brand's legacy is less about monuments or physical reminders and more about creating value, connections, and stories that endure. Social media offers an unprecedented opportunity to craft this kind of legacy, but doing so requires intention, consistency, and a forward-looking mindset.

Creating an archive of successful campaigns provides a foundation for future strategies. This practice goes beyond saving screenshots or storing posts—it's about curating a library of what worked, why it worked, and how it can inspire future ideas. For example, if a campaign featuring user-generated content drove exceptional engagement, documenting the steps that led to its success can serve as a blueprint for similar efforts later. An archive also helps identify patterns in audience preferences, allowing you to adapt over time without losing sight of your brand's core identity. **By treating past successes as a resource, you can keep your strategy grounded while experimenting with fresh ideas.**

Consistency is a cornerstone of building brand equity. The most memorable brands are those that deliver a cohesive message, tone, and aesthetic across all their channels, year after year. Social media algorithms and audience behaviors may change, but the value of a consistent presence remains constant. Think about Coca-Cola's unwavering commitment to happiness or Nike's focus on empowerment—each message adds to their brand equity. For smaller brands, this means aligning every post, comment, and interaction with your values and voice. **Every consistent interaction reinforces trust, making your brand a familiar and reliable presence in a crowded digital space.**

Planning for future growth is the next step in ensuring your social media efforts are not just reactive but proactive. As your audience expands, their needs and expectations will evolve. A small local audience might value direct engagement and personal touches, while a larger, more diverse following could require broader campaigns and more sophisticated tools. Thinking ahead means preparing for these shifts, whether by exploring new platforms, investing in tools to scale your efforts, or training team members to manage increased demand. **By anticipating growth, you can build a strategy that remains effective no matter how your audience changes.**

David Meerman Scott's insights in *The New Rules of Marketing and PR* emphasize the importance of aligning your efforts with an ever-changing digital landscape. He argues that lasting success depends on flexibility and a commitment to creating authentic, valuable content. This lesson resonates when considering social media legacy—it's not just about what you've done but about your readiness to adapt and stay relevant. Brands that fail to evolve risk becoming relics, while those that embrace change continue to grow their influence and impact.

Building a legacy on social media is about more than accumulating likes and shares. It's about establishing a presence that transcends fleeting trends, creating value that resonates with audiences over time. By documenting your successes, maintaining consistency, and preparing for growth, you can ensure that your efforts today lay the groundwork for a lasting and meaningful impact.

CHEAPTRIVIA.COM

BOOST REVENUE WITH TRIVIA

Revitalize Your Bar or Restaurant with Thrilling Trivia Nights!

- **Weekly trivia questions & answers**
- Boost revenue by thousands
- Enhance customer retention and loyalty
- **Social Posts and Posters available**
- Continuous customer service and support

CONCLUSION

Social media has become the modern restaurant's most powerful tool—not just for attracting attention but for building lasting relationships. It's not enough to serve great food anymore; diners want to feel connected, seen, and valued. When you implement the strategies outlined in this book, you're not just gaining followers or likes; you're cultivating a community around your brand. The true magic of social media lies in its ability to transform casual customers into passionate advocates, and that starts with showing up authentically and consistently.

Picture a bustling dining room filled with guests who first discovered your restaurant online. Maybe they came because they saw a beautifully plated dish on Instagram or watched a behind-the-scenes TikTok featuring your chef crafting a signature recipe. Maybe it was a heartfelt reply to their comment that made them feel like more than just another customer. Each interaction, each post, and each moment of engagement adds to the story you're telling, one that people want to be part of.

Of course, success in this space isn't about perfection—it's about progress. Even the most polished campaigns require trial and error, and the digital landscape is always shifting. What works today might not tomorrow, but that's what makes social media so exciting. You've learned how to define your goals, choose the right platforms, and measure your impact. With those foundations in place, you can adapt, evolve, and thrive no matter what changes come your way.

Think back to the examples shared in this book. The small café that partnered with local influencers to double its weekend reservations. The neighborhood diner that turned negative reviews into opportunities for improvement and loyalty. The upscale bistro that leveraged TikTok to make fine dining feel approachable to a new generation. These aren't exceptions—they're proof that with the right approach, any restaurant can use social media to drive real results.

And let's not forget the stories that diners share. Whether it's a quick snapshot of a meal or a heartfelt caption about their favorite dish, user-generated content amplifies your reach in ways advertising never could. Encouraging and celebrating those stories creates a ripple effect. One happy customer can inspire dozens more to visit, all because they felt a connection that extended beyond the plate.

It's easy to get caught up in the numbers: followers, likes, clicks. But the most important metric is the one that can't always be measured—the sense of trust and loyalty you create with your audience. When people feel like they know you, they're more likely to choose you, recommend you, and return time and time again. That's the kind of relationship that can weather competition, trends, and even the occasional misstep.

Building this kind of presence isn't about having the biggest budget or the fanciest tools. It's about authenticity, creativity, and a willingness to listen. Social media isn't a megaphone; it's a conversation. The restaurants that succeed are the ones that take the time to connect with their audience, respond to their needs, and share their stories in meaningful ways.

You now have the tools, insights, and strategies to make that happen. Whether it's crafting scroll-stopping content, navigating paid campaigns, or turning feedback into fuel for growth, you're equipped to not just survive in the digital age but to thrive. The next step is yours to take, and the possibilities are as exciting as the meals you serve.

At its heart, social media is about more than marketing. It's about celebrating what makes your restaurant special, creating moments that resonate, and sharing your passion with the world. By embracing these principles, you're not just building an online presence; you're building a brand that people love, trust, and can't wait to experience again.

Turn casual diners into loyal fans with Do Social Smarter's proven system to grow your customer base, boost reviews, and drive foot traffic effortlessly.

Visit DoSocialSmarter.com today and discover how to keep your seats full and your competition behind.

DO SOCIAL SMARTER, LLC

marketing   est. 2017

www.ingramcontent.com/pod-product-compliance
Lightning Source LLC
Chambersburg PA
CBHW071653240526
45469CB00023B/2298